D0582809

Nelson
MANDELA

WHO WAS...

This edition published in 2004 by
Short Books
15 Highbury Terrace
London N5 1UP

10 9 8 7 6 5 4 3 2 1

First published in Great Britain by Short Books Ltd in 2003

A CIP catalogue record for this book
is available from the British Library.

ISBN 1-904095-86-0

Printed in Great Britain by
Bookmarque Ltd, Croydon, Surrey

For Jackie, my wife and muse

CHAPTER ONE

Pretoria prison, South Africa, 1964: Nelson Mandela lay awake on his hard prison bed, staring at the ceiling. It was after midnight but he couldn't sleep. He thought about the day over and over again. He could still see the judge arriving in the court room, sitting down and nodding towards him as the court orderly said, 'All rise'. He could still feel what it was like to be standing there with his friends, waiting to hear if he was to live or die.

Nelson was sure it would be death. He had no doubt he would be taken away and hanged by the neck. He said to himself that if he was to die, it would be with courage. Every day for almost a year, the evil, dark shape of the gallows had lurked at the back of his mind: he could almost hear the creak of the thick rope looped at the end, as it swung to-and-fro above the trapdoor. He tried not to think about it. He tried not to imagine what it would be like to feel the rope put around his neck by an executioner or the sudden plunge through the trapdoor into darkness and death. But, however much he tried, the thoughts just wouldn't go away. It was as if wherever he went, he walked in the shadow of the gallows. And the prison warders took delight in reminding him of the fact. At night they would wake him up, saying: 'Hey Mandela, wake up. You don't have to worry about sleep. You are soon going to sleep for a long, long time.'

The question gnawed at his mind constantly like a rat nibbling a piece of cheese. Would he live or would he die? It was a terrible thing not to know. Nelson often thought of a saying he had read once. 'Better to assume you will die. For if you live, life will be sweeter. And if you are to die, you will be better prepared.' Nelson assumed the worst.

Now the moment had arrived. The judge shuffled his papers. Nelson watched the judge's every movement hoping for a sign. He tried to catch the judge's eye, but the judge avoided looking at him. He noticed the judge looked pale. He was also breathing heavily. Something was wrong. The judge was always so calm. Now he looked nervous. Nelson turned to his friends in the dock. They also noticed the judge was behaving strangely. Then they knew. It would be death.

The judge cleared his throat with a cough and began to speak. The packed courtroom went very, very quiet. Nelson held his breath. 'I have decided,' the judge said, reading from his notes, 'not to impose the supreme penalty.' The courtroom erupted. People sang and cheered. Many didn't even hear the verdict, including the families of the accused. One of Nelson's friends in the dock, Dennis Goldberg, saw his wife mouth the question: 'Dennis, what is it?'.

'Life,' he shouted to her. 'Life! To Live!'

Instead of being hanged, Nelson and his friends would be sent to prison for the rest of their lives, which didn't seem so bad, compared to the gallows.

Nelson looked desperately for his wife, Winnie, in the crowded court. In the crush of people, he couldn't see her anywhere. He so badly wanted to see her face. Then a police officer tapped him on the shoulder and he was led off to the cells once more.

And now here he was, lying on his cold bunk. Pictures of the day ran through his mind. He began to think of the future. What will happen to me now? he wondered. Will I really spend the rest of my days surrounded by walls and bars? In the silence of the jail, he heard a distant metal door clang shut. Then footsteps. Then another door. The steps grew louder and louder. Finally, a voice close by called to him: 'Mandela, are you awake?' Nelson knew the voice. It belonged to a prison warder by the name of Colonel Aucamp.

'You are a lucky man,' the colonel sneered, with a twisted smile on his face. 'We are taking you to a place where you will have your freedom. You will be able to move about, you'll see the ocean and the sky, not just grey walls. Now collect your things. We leave in 15 minutes.'

But Nelson knew the colonel was taunting him. He knew he was not really to be freed, nor would he be able to wander about under the open skies or breathe the sea air. He knew exactly what the colonel meant. He was to be taken to a place they called The Island: Robben Island, probably the meanest, toughest, cruellest jail in the world.

Soon Nelson was standing in the corridor of the prison with six of his friends. Their names were Govan, Ahmed, Elias, Andrew, Walter and Raymond. Like

Nelson, they had been told they were going to jail for the rest of their lives. And like Nelson, they knew they had done nothing other than stand up for what they truly believed in.

Chained together, the seven prisoners were led through the cold maze of the prison. They were taken down long damp corridors and through a dozen heavy steel doors. The echoes of each door clanging shut rang in their ears. In the courtyard, a police van was waiting for them. They were quickly piled into it, the door bolted shut behind them.

Inside the police van, the men were in good spirits. They had not been sentenced to die. They had escaped the hangman's noose! Sitting on the dusty floor of the van, they talked excitedly about the last day of the trial. They relived the moment of the judgement, remembered their reactions. They even sang a little, as they bumped along in the darkness. They sang songs to give them hope and courage. They sang songs to take their thoughts away from the unknown fears of the night. They sang songs of freedom.

After less than an hour, the van stopped. Outside, the night was cold and the sky filled with stars. Nelson saw they had arrived at a small military airport outside

Pretoria. Heavily-armed police officers, prison warders and soldiers watched nervously as the seven friends climbed out of the police van, shuffled across the tarmac of the airstrip still in their heavy iron chains and climbed into the back of the old Dakota airplane which awaited them.

The pilot fired up the engine and the Dakota's two big propellers began to turn. Once the propellers had built up enough speed and blurred into two big white circles, the old plane taxied to the start of the runway, paused, then sped down the tarmac. It climbed slowly into the night sky and turned to the south east. There was no heating in the plane and the seven friends shivered in the cold. A couple of the men had never flown before. They were frightened. They looked at the shuddering metal tube and tried not to think about the thousands of feet of empty space opening up between them and the ground.

It wasn't long before dawn began to lighten the sky. Through the portholes, the men could see the edges of the night turn from inky black to royal blue. Nelson leaned over and pushed his face against the cold glass. Far below, the dry, flat plains of the Orange Free State curled up into the towering green mountains of the

Cape. He could see farms and small towns, rivers and roads. The Dakota rumbled high over the city of Cape Town, which sits right at the very tip of southern Africa, perched on a jagged peninsula and surrounded by deep, blue ocean. The city's people shelter from the storms and the fierce winds at the stone feet of a huge, flat-topped mountain, called Table Mountain.

As the sun crept over the apricot horizon, Mandela caught sight of the city. He was then able to make out the place where they were going. About 11 miles off the coast from Cape Town, covered in a thin blanket of sea mist, was Robben Island.

The Dakota crept lower and lower, dropping through the low cloud toward the torch-lit landing strip. After a bone-jarring bump, the airplane settled and braked to a standstill. Through the porthole, Mandela could see dozens of guards with automatic weapons waiting in the shadows. It was a grim, overcast day and, as the prisoners stepped out of the plane, a biting winter wind whipped through their thin regulation uniforms. It was so cold it made their bones ache. Not far from the airstrip was a one-storey, rectangular stone fortress, which had been built specially for Nelson and his friends. The ordinary criminals lived in a much bigger prison further down the road.

The fortress for the political prisoners was patrolled by guards with ill-tempered Alsatian dogs. In its centre was a concrete courtyard. Nelson was ordered to change into a new set of khaki prison clothes. He was given sandals made from rubber tyres and shorts even though it was freezing cold. He was taken to what was called Section B, a row of cells earmarked for political leaders which overlooked the courtyard. His cell was towards one end of the corridor and had a white card posted outside saying 'NR Mandela 466/64'. He was the 466th prisoner to arrive on Robben Island in the year 1964.

The cell had two doors. The first door was a heavy wooden one. Inside that was a grille of iron bars. There was a rolled up straw mat in one corner which was Nelson's bed. At night he would open it out and put it on the concrete floor. Three paper thin blankets were all he was given for warmth. A one-foot-square window lined by bars as thick as a grown-up's wrist overlooked the courtyard. Nelson could walk from one side of the cell to the other in three paces. If he lay down on the straw mat, his head touched one wall and his feet touched the other. The walls were three feet thick and were damp to the touch. Even with the window closed, the cell was always cold.

Nelson was 46 years old. His wife and children were a thousand miles away. He had lost his freedom and his future. In fact this little, cold, grey room would be his home for the next 18 years. But the amazing thing is that even if Nelson had known he would end up in prison, he wouldn't have done anything differently. He regretted none of the decisions which had landed him on Robben Island; he knew he had done the right thing. To understand why he felt as he did, we have to go all the way back to the year 1918, back to a small African village on the banks of the Mbashe (pronounced Bashee) River.

CHAPTER TWO

Chief Gadla Henry Mandela was an important man in the village of Mvezo. In those days in Africa, the more important a man was, the more wives he had. Chief Mandela had four wives, each with their own *kraal*. A *kraal* is a homestead consisting of several thatched huts, a fenced pen for animals and fields for crops like vegetables and corn. Chief Mandela had many cattle which was a sign of great wealth. Though he could neither read nor write, he was very wise. He also had a long, long memory. He remembered all the tales and lore of years long past. Sometimes he would tell stories around the fire in the evenings. He was a tall, dark-skinned man with a straight and stately posture as befitted a member of the Thembu royal family.

But, although he had royal blood, Chief Mandela was

not in direct line to the throne. Instead, he was a royal counsellor. His job was to give advice to the rulers of the Thembu people.

The Thembu are a proud people who live in a small area the size of Switzerland on the east coast of the country of South Africa. The Thembu are part of the Xhosa nation who in turn are part of the Nguni people. The Nguni have lived, hunted, farmed and fished in the south-eastern region of Africa since at least the eleventh century. Their history is littered with stories of great kings and queens, warriors and prophets, heroes and villains. Their tales are full of magic, great feats, battles and adventures. For centuries, there was little more precious to the Thembu than justice, fairness and respect for the law.

On July 18 of the year 1918, Chief Mandela's third wife, Nosekeni Fanny, gave birth to a son. The son was given the name Rolihlahla, which literally means 'he who pulls the branch of a tree', but which really means 'trou-blemaker'. This was to prove an apt name for the small child. Later, when he went to school, the child was given the name 'Nelson' by his teacher. All African children at that time were given western 'Christian' names. His teacher never explained why she chose

'Nelson', but it was probably after the legendary English admiral, Horatio Nelson.

Not long after Nelson was born, his father had a bitter argument with the local magistrate (a court judge). In those days, the magistrates wielded great power even over kings and chiefs. Nelson's father was stripped of his chieftaincy. His lands and his cattle were taken away. He was suddenly a poor man and could no longer afford to keep four wives and 13 children. He sent Nosekeni Fanny and her three children to live with her relatives in a nearby village.

It was here in a tiny country hamlet called Qunu (the 'Q' is pronounced by making a kind of click sound with your tongue), 500 miles from the nearest city, where Nelson spent his boyhood years. They were wonderful, simple, happy years. Later, when he was sad in jail, he often thought back to them. He remembered the beautiful rolling hills that were always green and the swims in freezing streams. He licked his lips recalling the fish he and his friends caught with a string and a piece of wire and laughed at how he drank warm milk straight from a cow's udder. How good that corn on the cob tasted freshly picked and roasted with sticks on an open fire!

Nelson lived with his mother and two sisters in a

kraal made up of three mud huts shaped like beehives. In one hut, the family cooked. In one they slept. And in the last hut they kept the food. All the huts had peaked roofs of grass held together with rope and propped up with a wooden pole. There were no beds or tables, only mats for sitting on or for sleeping. The stove was a hole in the ground and the cupboard was mud moulded into shape like a sandcastle.

In Africa, the ants make houses out of mud that are called antheaps. They are often as tall as a grown-up, shaped liked a pointed witch's hat, and sometimes the ants build them under a tree for shade. They take many years to build, piece by tiny piece. And this means the mud is very fine, with no big lumps at all. Many years ago, someone in Africa had realised that if you mixed crushed antheap mud with cow dung, you could make a smooth, cool surface perfect for the floor of a hut. Nelson's home had a floor just like it, which was kept smooth with a regular smearing of fresh cow dung.

Meals when Nelson was a boy were cooked in a three-legged metal pot. Supper was usually corn ground into a powder and mixed with sour milk. Sometimes the family had pumpkins or beans and, on really special occasions, some meat. The family took their main meal together sitting on the ground and eating from a single dish.

There were no roads in the village, only paths worn through the grass by bare feet. The women and children didn't wear clothes in the western sense, only blankets dyed in red ochre. There was no running water or electricity, and there were certainly no televisions or computers. From the age of five, Nelson was given the important job of herd boy. He looked after the cattle, sheep and goats in the fields. When he wasn't tending the livestock, he was running in the fields or fighting his friends with sticks. Stick-fighting, in which a long stick is held in each hand like a sword, was a skill every Thembu boy learned from an early age. It taught them many a painful lesson in guile, swiftness and concentration.

Riding the naughty village donkey was another thing the boys loved to do. They liked to show how brave they were by jumping on and off the donkey's back. One day, the boys were playing with the grumpy donkey and it was Nelson's turn to climb on its back. As soon as he jumped on, the donkey bolted and ran straight into a nearby thornbush. Nelson's face was scratched and bleeding from the thorns. His friends laughed at him so hard they could barely stand. Nelson learned an important lesson that day. He learned there is nothing worse than feeling humiliated. Winning is one thing, but making someone suffer is cruel. It was a lesson that would mean a great deal to him many years in the future.

Nelson's father used to travel between the *kraals* of his four wives, staying a few days at each. During one visit, when Nelson was nine years old, he noticed his father was not looking at all well. He coughed badly and seemed very weak. Before the sun had risen the next morning, Chief Mandela was dead. This made Nelson very sad. He had loved his father. Chief Mandela had had a grey streak in his hair and sometimes Nelson used to rub cold ash from the fire on to his head to pretend he was the big proud chief with the grey streak. What would happen to Nelson now the chief was gone?

Shortly after Chief Mandela's death, Nelson's mother told him to pack his things as they would be leaving the next morning. Nelson only had a few possessions: a sling to shoot birds, clay models of cows and sheep he had made himself and a precious pair of trousers. The trousers had been given to him by his father on his first day of school. They had belonged to Chief Mandela and simply been cut at the knee. They were much too big but

Nelson kept them up with a piece of string. He would never be prouder in any suit than he was in his father's cut-off trousers.

Nosekeni Fanny woke up Nelson early and together they set off. At the crest of the hill, Nelson turned and looked back at the village. How he loved Qunu and especially the three beehive huts that were his home! He wondered what his friends were doing and if he would ever see this place again. Then he turned and they walked on. He didn't know where he was going and didn't ask.

Mother and son walked in silence all day. They clambered along rocky paths, trudged up and down hills and went past many villages. Finally, as the sun sank close to the horizon, they came to a shallow valley surrounded by trees. There, next to a cornfield bordered by peach trees, lay a grand house. The walls of the house were washed in white lime which dazzled in the light of the setting sun.

Nelson had never seen anything like it. He saw many fields, apple trees, vegetable gardens, at least 50 cows and hundreds of sheep. Near to the grand house there was a white stucco church. In the shade of two bluegum trees a group of elders sat together in the fading light.

This was the Great Place, the palace of the Thembu people. And this was where Nelson had been brought to live, to take his place as a prince in the royal household.

CHAPTER THREE

Chief Joyi was so old his wrinkled skin hung off his bones like a loose-fitting coat. Or so it seemed to Nelson. Sometimes he would cough for minutes at a time, his face going bright red. But in spite of his age and his cough, nobody could tell stories like he could. He brought ancient tales so alive it really felt as though you were there.

As Nelson watched... the chief crept through the grass, spear in hand. Here was the hero leading his army. The enemy was close by. A great battle was looming. As the chief crouched, waiting, his hushed words told the story. Suddenly, the old chief leaped into the air. The audience gasped. The old chief thrust his spear this way and that. The battle was won. He shouted and stamped his feet. Everyone clapped and cheered. For young

Nelson, there was no better way in the world to spend the hours before bed than sitting by a crackling fire beneath the bluegum trees listening to Chief Joyi.

The old chief was especially cross with the 'White Man' who had come across the sea and divided the Xhosa nation. But Nelson didn't pay much attention to that. He didn't really know what the old chief meant. He was much more interested in the heroes like Makanna and Autshumao.

Makanna was the giant, six-foot-six commander of the Xhosa army who led 10,000 warriors against Grahamstown in 1819. Autshumao, or 'Henry the Strandloper' as the history books call him, was the chief of the Khoi Khoi people who fought the Dutch in the 17th century. The Khoi Khoi have lived on the southern tip of Africa for a long, long time. Some say they were the first human beings anywhere and that we are all descended from them. Both Makanna and Autshumao were eventually caught and banished to a narrow, windswept outcrop of rock off the coast of Cape Town called Robben Island.

Even as a child, Nelson had heard the tales about the terrible Robben Island. Even then he knew that very few people had ever escaped from the island and lived. Not even great Xhosa warriors. But the tales made Nelson's heart swell with pride. Here were African heroes, his forbears and kinsmen, doing brave and wondrous things. He learned that there were many African tribes and each had its kings, its battles and its stories.

Nelson learned a great deal during his years at the Great Place.

He discovered that he had been brought to the palace after being adopted by the regent of the Thembu people. The future king, Sabata, was still too young to rule, so a regent had been put in place to look after things until he grew up. The regent had been a friend of Nelson's father and had agreed, on Chief Mandela's death, to take Nelson into his home and treat him as one of his own children.

And so Nelson was accepted into the Great Place of the Thembu as a son of the regent. He was a prince and the Thembu people treated him as one. Instead of sharing a mud hut with his mother and two sisters, Nelson lived in a plastered, round cottage with the regent's own son, Justice. The cottage had wooden floorboards, something Nelson had never seen before. He had his own bed for the first time.

Nelson and Justice, who was four years older than

Nelson, became best friends. They roamed the fields and gardens of the Great Place together. When they were not in school, they rode horses, helped to plough the fields and sucked on honeycombs plucked straight from beehives. Even Nelson's chores were an adventure in this magical kingdom. One of his favourite duties was pressing the regent's suits so the creases were as sharp as the edge of a warrior's spear.

It was at the Great Place that Nelson saw a motor car for the first time: a majestic Ford V8 driven by the regent. He got used to wearing western clothes and was given his first pair of shiny boots. It was also at the Great Place that Nelson began to learn the lessons that were expected, one day, to help him advise the future Thembu King, Sabata.

One of the things Nelson liked best was to attend the meetings of the Thembu council of elders. When something important happened in Thembu Land – like a new tax or an outbreak of cattle disease – a tribal meeting, or council of elders, was called at the Great Place. All Thembus were free to attend. Some rode to the meeting on horses or donkeys. Some walked for many days from the far reaches of the Thembu kingdom. There were always lots of people and the meetings could go on for hours and hours. A big feast was served during the day, usually of a roasted ox and several sheep. Nelson often gave himself a nasty bellyache by eating much too much. He just couldn't help himself. It was all so delicious and there were so many people to listen to.

The regent always began these councils the same way. First, he thanked everyone for coming so far. He explained why they had been called. Then he sat down and didn't say another word until right at the end. For the rest of the time, every Thembu person who wanted to speak did so. Whoever they were, whether a shopkeeper or a king, a shepherd or a farmer, their voice was heard. When everyone had had their turn, the regent spoke once more. Sometimes, everybody agreed on what to do. Sometimes they didn't. If they couldn't decide, they planned to have another meeting to discuss things further. In this way, the Thembu people took all their important decisions together.

At first, Nelson went to a school near to the Great Place. He studied English, history, the Xhosa language and geography. He did his lessons on black slates with chalk. After a while, he was sent to a boarding school 60 miles away to join Justice at a place called the Clarkebury Institute. This school, like many of the best schools in Africa at that time, was a mission school. That means they were started by missionaries who wanted to teach Christianity and other lessons to African children. Clarkebury was a Methodist mission school run by a stern principal by the name of Reverend Harris.

When Nelson arrived at Clarkebury, he expected his fellow students and even his teachers to treat him like a prince. He was surprised when this didn't happen. Hardly anyone knew or cared about his royal blood. Each person was treated according to how they behaved and not according to who they were or where they came from. This was another important lesson for Nelson.

After classes, the students were required to work in the school grounds each day for several hours. Nelson chose to work in the garden of the principal. Two things happened in the garden. First, he developed a passion for gardening and especially for the growing of vegetables. He loved to plant the seeds, tending to them as they grew and then harvesting them when they were just right. Second, he came to know the Harris family. The Harrises were the first white people with whom Nelson had ever spent time. He liked them very much. There were not that many white people in the Thembu kingdom, and the few that there were were mostly travellers, police officers and government officials whom Nelson had only ever seen very occasionally. The local magistrate in Qunu had been a white person. So too was the nearest shopkeeper. Beyond these brief encounters, Nelson's only experience of white people was in the tales and songs of the Thembu. As a child, white people had seemed as grand as gods to him. Seeing them conjured feelings of fear and respect, they were people of authority, as alien to Nelson's world as they were powerful within it.

Reverend Harris and his wife were the first white people with whom Nelson shook hands. Once he got to know them, they proved far removed from the fantasies of Nelson's youth. Reverend Harris ruled the school with an iron fist, but in private, he was a quiet, kind and gentle man. His wife was as talkative as the Reverend was thoughtful, and she often chatted to Nelson for what seemed like hours. Nelson would never forget the warm scones Mrs Harris brought out to him in the garden in the afternoons.

Nelson did not think he was clever at school. But he worked very hard and, like his father, he had a fine memory. He grew to love long-distance running and also boxing and he became quite good at both. He soon moved to college and then, at the age of 21, to the University of Fort Hare in a town called Alice. The university had been built by Scottish missionaries in 1916 on the site of an old fort. It sat at the end of a winding road on a rocky platform overlooking a green valley. Around it bubbled and gushed the Tyume River. For young black South Africans like Nelson, it was Oxford and Cambridge rolled into one. More than a thousand students were housed and taught in the university's ivy-covered buildings. The students paused to chat between lessons in tree-shaded courtyards.

Slowly, Nelson's horizons were stretching. As he would say later, once you have climbed one hill, there is always another one, and then another. As a small boy he had wanted nothing more than to eat well and to be the champion stick-fighter of his village. As a young man, he hoped to do well at school, find a good job and then take up his duties as counsellor to King Sabata. But the more new people he met, the more stories he heard and the more educated he became, the more Nelson dreamed of bigger things. He dreamed of crossing great rivers and visiting faraway cities. He dreamed of finding a beautiful wife and of wearing fine clothes. He and Justice learned ballroom dancing, wore double-breasted suits and talked of what was happening in the world. In 1939, when Nelson was still at university, a world war broke out. The world was changing and Nelson's eyes were opening.

At the university, the tall and princely Nelson was chosen by his classmates to represent them on the student council. The food at the university was horrible and they wanted Nelson and the rest of the council to do something about it. Nelson's fight to improve the food landed him in hot water with the principal. Nelson was told he would have to leave the university if he continued. But, for the first time, Nelson realised what it was like to stand up for what he believed in. Being on the 'right' side gave him a feeling of strength and power. It also got him into trouble.

One day, the regent called Nelson and Justice to come and see him. He told the surprised young men that he was dying. 'I am not much longer for this world,' he said. 'But before I journey to the land of the ancestors, it is my duty to see my two sons properly married. I have, accordingly, arranged unions for both of you.'

Nelson and Justice looked at each other in shock. They didn't want to get married. Not yet anyway. They didn't even like the two young women the regent had chosen for them. For Justice, the regent had selected the daughter of a well-respected Thembu nobleman. For Nelson, the regent had agreed on the daughter of the local Thembu priest. Nelson thought the young woman intended for him was dignified but he didn't think she was beautiful. He also knew she was in love with Justice and had been for ages.

'The marriages will take place immediately,' the regent told them. In traditional Thembu custom, it was quite normal for parents to arrange marriages. But Nelson and Justice felt they had moved on from this. They thought they were modern young men and did not want to obey the rules of tradition. They wanted to fall in love. They wanted to marry women who won their hearts, not the women their father had chosen for them.

That night, Nelson and Justice decided to run away. They had heard from their friends about a city of gold many days' travel away. They agreed that the next day they would head for the big city. They decided to wait for the regent to leave the Great Place in his car. Then they would make a run for it.

CHAPTER FOUR

As the morning sun crept over the fields of the Great Place, Nelson and Justice packed their few things into one small, shared suitcase. It was a Monday and they knew the regent was leaving early on a trip that would keep him away for a whole week. They smiled at each other when they heard the gruff engine of the Ford V8 cough into life. Soon, the car drove up the dirt road with a cloud of red dust behind it and disappeared. The regent was gone.

Nelson and Justice went over their plan. They popped down the road to a cattle trader and sold two of the regent's prize oxen. The trader didn't suspect a thing. They now had enough money to pay for their trip to the city. Back at the Great Place, they decided the hour had come. It was mid-morning and the regent had been gone for several hours. The car they had hired to pick them up and deliver them to the local train station was due any minute.

They were pleased when, right on time, they heard the noise of an engine coming down the road leading into the valley. But it wasn't their car. It was the regent. He was coming back. Nelson and Justice didn't know what to do. They looked at each other in terror. If the regent saw them in their best clothes with a suitcase, he would know for sure that something was up. They ran into the corn field and hid, quiet as field mice.

'Where are those boys?' they heard the regent shout as soon as he had climbed out of his car.

'Oh, they are around somewhere,' replied one of the elders, sitting under the bluegum tree. The regent huffed. He went into the main house.

'Bring me my indigestion tablets,' they heard him call out loudly. That was why the regent had returned. But both Nelson and Justice knew the regent could have bought tablets for his tummy anywhere in town. The regent must suspect something, they thought.

After a little look around the house, the regent climbed back into his car. Justice and Nelson could hardly bear to look. But soon, he was zooming up the valley road and quickly disappeared behind the hills. When he was gone, Nelson and Justice breathed a huge sigh of relief. That was close. Just then, another car came down the road. Not the regent again, they wondered? No. This time, it was the car they had hired. After the small hiccough, they were off on their trip once more.

The car took the two young men to the station where they hoped to catch a train to Johannesburg, a city which in Xhosa is called 'Egoli', 'City of Gold'.

'Could we have two tickets to Johannesburg,' Nelson asked at the counter.

'Please wait a minute,' replied the clerk, who climbed off his stool and left the office. A moment later, the station manager arrived.

'We cannot sell you tickets so please go home,' the manager told Nelson and Justice.

'Why ever not?' asked Justice, 'we have the money'.

'Your father was here earlier this morning,' the station manager said. 'He says you are trying to run away.'

Nelson and Justice were dismayed. They left the station and, luckily, their car was still outside. 'Take us to the next station,' they cried.

'But it's more than 50 miles away,' replied the driver.

'That doesn't matter,' said Justice. 'Take us.'

So the driver took the young men to the next station and they boarded the first train. It was only going as far as Queenstown, which was still a long, long way from Johannesburg. But it was a start, at least.

Once they were on the train, Justice and Nelson tried to figure out a plan. 'What are we going to do for travel papers?' asked Nelson.

At that time, all Africans over the age of 16 needed special passes to travel from one town to the next. Any policeman, official or employer could demand to see the pass. If you didn't have a pass, you could be arrested and put in jail. White people did not need a pass.

As well as the pass, Africans also needed travel papers. These included a travel permit and a letter from an employer or from a parent or guardian. Nelson and Justice had passes, but not travel papers. To be caught without them meant big trouble. Even if you had all the right papers, the police could still make life very unpleasant over the smallest thing. If the date was wrong or a signature was missing, you could be thrown in jail. White people didn't need travel papers.

Justice and Nelson planned to go to the house of a relative in Queenstown to try to get their travel papers from there. As luck would have it, the two young men found a friendly uncle at the house who said he would help them. The kind uncle took Justice and Nelson to the office of a magistrate whom he knew well. 'We are on a special errand for the regent,' Justice lied to the magistrate.

The magistrate knew the regent and had no reason to doubt their story. He did wonder why they hadn't got the right papers. But he made out the necessary documents and with a clunk, gave it the official stamp. Luck was smiling on the two princes and they knew it. But just as he was handing over the documents, the magistrate remembered that to be polite, he should call his fellow magistrate from the town nearest the Great Place. He dialled the number and explained what he had done.

'There's no need to tell me,' said the local magistrate. 'The regent is here in my office. You can tell him yourself.' The phone was handed to the regent and the magistrate from Queenstown told him about the brothers' request for travel papers.

'Arrest those boys!' the regent shouted so loud that

Nelson and Justice could hear it through the phone receiver.

Both the magistrate and their uncle were very cross.

'You are thieves and liars,' the magistrate shouted, 'and you are under arrest.'

Nelson stood up and looked the magistrate in the eye. 'I'm sorry, sir, but you may not arrest us,' he said.

'And why not?' asked the magistrate icily.

'Because I have studied law and I know that you cannot arrest us merely because a chief says so, even if that chief is our father.'

'As it happens, you are right,' replied the magistrate. 'I cannot arrest you. But I want you to leave and never darken my door again. Now get out!'

Justice and Nelson grabbed their suitcase and dashed out of the magistrate's office.

'Now what are we going to do?' asked Nelson.

'Don't worry, Nelson. I've got a plan,' said Justice. Nelson rolled his eyeballs: so far, Justice's plans had not worked very well.

The two young men walked into Queenstown to the office of a local lawyer. Justice had a friend called Sidney who worked in the office. 'Sidney, we need your help,' said Justice. 'We need to get to Johannesburg.'

'You are lucky,' Sidney said. 'The mother of the man I work for is driving to Johannesburg early tomorrow morning. She might be able to take you, for a fee.'

'Fine, fine,' said Justice. 'We are willing to pay'.

When they heard how much the woman wanted to charge them, they nearly fell off their chairs. She wanted £15. In the 1940s, that was a great deal of money. It was almost all the money they had made from selling two of the regent's prized oxen. But they had no other choice, and knew it.

'Okay, okay, we'll take it,' said Justice.

Justice, Nelson and the lawyer's mother left early the next morning. As was usual at that time, the two black men sat in the back of the car and the white lady sat in the front. The old lady kept a close eye on the two young men through her rear view mirror. She clearly didn't trust them, and she kept an especially close watch on Justice who chattered non-stop. She wasn't used to black men who felt free to chat and laugh in the company of an old white woman. She thought young black men should sit quietly and wait until they were spoken to.

At about ten o'clock that evening. Justice and Nelson saw the city of Johannesburg, glinting in the distance. As they got nearer the city began to look like a vast blanket of lights stretching in all directions. For two country boys who rarely saw electricity, the burning lights of the city were like a dream. The night sky glowed with gold and silver. They had heard stories about the city and scarcely believed them; they had heard that there were people who spoke languages you had never heard of and buildings so tall you couldn't see the top of them. They stared in awe at the huge billboards advertising cigarettes and beer. Here was the city they had heard so much about, the city of sleek motor cars, beautiful women and dashing gangsters. Here, at last, was Johannesburg, the city of gold.

CHAPTER FIVE

Nelson and Justice arrived in Johannesburg in the autumn of 1941. Nelson was 22 years old. There were many others, young and old, who were also making their way to the city at that time. They came from villages and towns from one end of the nation to the other. They even came from neighbouring countries. All of them were looking for new lives, for money and jobs and for the excitement of the big city. Many still dressed in the blankets they wore in their villages. Others were dressed in smart suits. Quite a few had been to school or university and had high hopes.

But back then Johannesburg was a cruel, tough place especially for young black men seeking their fortune. There were many, many rules and laws which made life very difficult and even more unfair.

Black people could only live in certain areas. These places, or townships, were mostly a long way out of the city. They were often dirty, dark places without running water or electricity. The houses were made of pieces of cardboard, wood and junk.

And black people could only take certain kinds of jobs, usually low-paid jobs like cleaning or manual labour. Many young black men worked in the gold mines of Johannesburg. The gold mines were the reason Johannesburg had been built and the city was littered with huge, 100-foot-high oblong piles of earth which had been dug out of the mines. These piles were called mine dumps and the earth in them still had a golden tint. The city thrived on the gold and even looked golden. No wonder it was called the city of gold.

Nelson and Justice went to one of the big gold mines to try to get work. But it wasn't long before the mine managers learned that they had run away and asked them to leave. The managers didn't want to make the regent of Thembu Land angry because many of the miners came from there. For a short time, Nelson worked as a mine policeman, but he was soon kicked out of his job. The regent kept sending messages pleading for Justice and Nelson to come home. Eventually, Justice did go home. But Nelson was determined to stay on.

Before long, a cousin of Nelson's sent him to meet a man called Walter Sisulu. Walter was a city-wise, fast-talking estate agent. He liked Nelson immediately. When Nelson told Walter he wanted to become a lawyer, Walter sent him to see someone in town who he thought might be able to help. The man's name was Lazar Sidelsky and he was a lawyer. Mr Sidelsky liked Nelson, too, and agreed to let him work as a clerk in his office, although this was very unusual as lawyers did not usually hire black clerks.

Nelson worked in the law firm during the day. At night he studied to become a lawyer. 'Stay out of politics,' his new boss warned him. 'It will only get you into trouble'.

Nelson lived in a township called Alexandra, which was nicknamed the Dark City. It was about six miles from the centre of Johannesburg and had no running water or electricity. There were a few brick houses, but most people lived in shacks.

It was dirty, noisy and dangerous. Criminals and gangsters roamed the streets. Mandela rented a small backroom and often walked the 12 miles to and from work to save on his bus fare. He worked on his law books in the evenings by the light of a paraffin lamp. Sometimes he went for days at a time without food because he didn't have enough money. He only had one suit, which his boss Sidelsky had given him. He wore it until it was threadbare.

These were hard days for Nelson. They were also wonderful times. He met some amazing people who taught him much about life in his country. Walter became a life-long friend. So too did a man called Oliver Tambo, who was also training to be a lawyer. Nelson saw that black people were treated very differently to white people in South Africa. White people didn't need a pass. They didn't need travel papers. They could take any job and live in any part of the city. Their streets were kept cleaner and safer. They could send their children to any school they liked.

Black people, on the other hand, had more and more rules to obey. One of the rules was that they couldn't vote. This meant there were no black people in the government. As most people living in South Africa were black, this seemed odd and very unfair to Nelson. And he and his friends spent many hours wondering what they could do to make things better.

Then, in 1948, things suddenly got worse. A lot

worse. A new political party was elected to power, called the National Party. The official line was that this party had been 'democratically' elected, but of course only white people had been allowed to take part in the election.

The National Party was mainly made up of white people from a community called the Afrikaners. In South Africa at that time, there were two groups of white people, who over the years fought with one another for all sorts of reasons. One group was the 'English-speaking' whites who had sailed to South Africa mainly from the United Kingdom. The other group was the Afrikaners, who spoke a form of Dutch called Afrikaans. They were people of European descent who had fled from Holland and France and started to migrate to South Africa in the seventeenth century in order to establish a new homeland where they could practise their religion in peace. They had fought two wars against the British at the turn of the twentieth century and won both. They had also fought many wars with the black tribes who were already living in Africa when the Afrikaners arrived. When the Afrikaners finally achieved political power in 1948, they were determined to make sure that no-one ever told them what to do, not the British, not the English-speaking whites and not the black people.

They put in place many, many new rules to make sure of this. One rule was that a person's skin colour was the most important thing about them. It didn't matter if you were clever or stupid, rich or poor, friendly or ugly. If your skin was white, you were allowed to live in nice places, work in nice jobs and go to nice schools. And if you were black, you weren't.

Everything the National Party did was aimed at keeping white people separate from black people. This was called 'apartheid', which is an Afrikaans word meaning 'keeping people apart'. Black people were not allowed to marry white people, they weren't allowed to share the same bus or even buy food from the same shop. The idea was to make sure black people never felt at home in 'white' cities.

Some white people disagreed with this, but the vast majority liked the idea of 'apartheid' so much that it became the law of the land. Even though most of the people living in South Africa were black, they were treated the worst, given the least land, the nastiest jobs and the most horrible places to live. And how did the National Party ensure that nobody broke the rules or tried to change them? By training thousands of police officers and by building a big army with lots of tanks and guns. Nobody argued with tanks and guns – nobody who wanted to stay alive and out of prison.

Nelson looked on in amazement and anger as South Africa became a worse and worse country to live in for black people. He and his friends thought everyone should be treated the same way whether they were white or black. And so Nelson joined a political party which thought exactly along these lines. It was called the African National Congress (ANC). The ANC had been founded in 1912 and had already been fighting for more than 30 years to make things better for black people.

The ANC came up with lots of different ways of trying to persuade the National Party to change its mind and treat black people as equals. They refused to go to work. But that did no good. They marched through the streets singing and shouting. That didn't work either. They wrote letters. They complained. They appealed to Britain and to other countries round the world. They tried everything they could think of. Still the National Party wouldn't listen. Instead, the National Party got angrier and angrier. They didn't want black people and white people to be the same. They thought white people were better and more important. They even thought the Afrikaners were God's 'chosen people'. They sent police and troops to arrest and imprison anyone who argued with them.

Nelson was getting closer and closer to becoming a lawyer, but was finding it very hard. After completing his degree by post, he went to university in Johannesburg. As a black person, he was not allowed into the same restaurants to eat with his white fellow students. He was not allowed to use the university's sports fields or its tennis courts or even its swimming pool. He was not allowed on the same trains or even on the tram. And, after a hard day's work at the law firm, he had to go home at night to a dark shack.

Every day he was reminded that black people were thought to be inferior. It was like suffering a thousand pinpricks. It made Nelson really angry. He hated not being treated as Nelson, the proud Thembu prince, or even as Nelson the young professional. He was merely a black man in a country in which black people were not welcome. Worse yet: it was his country! Nelson was determined to change things.

One day at Walter's home, Nelson was introduced to a young woman by the name of Evelyn. Evelyn was

Walter's younger cousin and she worked as a nurse. Nelson and Evelyn fell in love. In 1944, they got married. At first the married couple shared a room in Evelyn's brother's house but they soon moved to a small three-roomed 'matchbox' house in a township called Orlando. It didn't have electricity or an inside lavatory but they loved their house anyway. It was the first house Nelson had ever owned and he was very proud of it.

A year after the wedding, Nelson and Evelyn had a son, Thembi. Then, the following year, they had a daughter, Makaziwe. Sadly, Makaziwe was sickly from birth and died after only nine months. Nelson and Evelyn then had another daughter who they also called Makaziwe. It is a common thing in Africa to give a child the name of a child who died. It is a sign of respect and remembrance.

While Nelson loved his family, his interest in politics grew by the day. It demanded more and more of his time. It also grew more and more dangerous. On the night of 1 May 1950, he and Walter were walking home to Orlando when they came across a group of people marching peacefully. May 1st is Workers' Day in many parts of the world. Suddenly, mounted police officers came clattering down the street. They started shooting.

Nelson and Walter hid in a nearby building. They later learned that 18 people were killed that night.

It was a turning point in Nelson's life. He learned that the police would stop at nothing to prevent black people from showing their unhappiness.

Nelson finally completed his training as a lawyer and in August 1952 he opened Johannesburg's first black legal practice with his friend Oliver Tambo. They put a sign in the window saying: 'MANDELA AND TAMBO, ATTORNEYS AT LAW'. There was always a big crowd in their office. Many people needed their help because there were so many rules that made life difficult for black people. Nelson felt that at last he was doing something to help.

Nelson became more and more popular and soon became one of the ANC's young leaders. He had become a tall man, just like his father. He walked and talked with all the grace and dignity of a Thembu prince. He loved boxing and was fit and agile. He also cared deeply for ordinary people.

Around that time, the ANC tried a new tactic. They used something which had worked quite well in India during that country's effort to win freedom from the British empire – something called defiance. The idea was that if enough people refused to obey the law, the prisons would become overcrowded and the government would see that the law was silly.

The ANC called their plan the Defiance Campaign. All at once, thousands of people broke the rules to say they had had enough. If no black people were allowed on a train, black people went on the train. If black people weren't allowed to swim in the public swimming pool, they did just that. More than 8,500 people of all races joined the campaign and every one of them was thrown into prison. Nelson led the campaign as the 'volunteer-in-chief'. He was arrested and spent several days in the police cells.

The government soon realised that Nelson was a troublemaker, just like his Thembu name suggested. They did all they could to make life hard for him. Later in the year they threw him in prison again. They made more laws and added more rules. Nelson was more determined than ever to change things. He believed with all his heart that his people, black South Africans, were not being fairly treated.

He went to many meetings and planned campaigns and protests with his friends. He worked long hours at the law practice. Soon his wife, Evelyn, complained.

She was a devout Jehovah's Witness and thought that Nelson should spend what little free time he had with his family or studying the Bible.

'You don't see us any more,' she said. Then she laid down an ultimatum: 'You must choose: either you resign from the ANC, or I will leave you, with our children.'

This was a very hard decision for Nelson. Who came first, his own family or his people? As much as it hurt him, he decided that he must choose his people. If he could change things, every child could look forward to a better future. If he chose to support only his family, his own children would see more of him but every child would suffer from apartheid, perhaps forever. He simply could not carry on with his own life as if nothing else was important. It was a great sacrifice but Nelson felt he had no choice.

Meanwhile, the authorities would not let up on him. The government told him that he wasn't allowed to leave Johannesburg. Then they told him that, for the next two years, he was not to meet with more than one other person at a time. This was called a banning order. Nelson was banned three times. Then, in 1956, he was charged with High Treason. If found guilty, the punishment for High Treason was death.

Evelyn could bear it no longer. When Nelson came home from the courtroom one night, he found the house empty. Evelyn had taken the children and the furniture. She had even taken the curtains. It was the saddest moment of Nelson's life. But he was determined to fight on. He was not fighting for himself. He was fighting for everybody.

CHAPTER SIX

The smart car turned on to the main route north out of the city of Johannesburg. At the wheel of the car was a chauffeur in a blue uniform. He wore a hat and round glasses and he had a bushy beard. The chauffeur drove slowly and carefully. Soon, he came to a suburb on the city outskirts called Rivonia. Here, he turned down a driveway and arrived at a small homestead called Liliesleaf Farm.

The chauffeur was Nelson. He was in disguise. It was the year 1962. Things had certainly changed in the last few years. The government had got so fed up with the ANC that it had closed the party down altogether; now you could be thrown in jail just for being a member of it. Many new laws had been passed; schools were even ordered to teach different things to black and white pupils. Because the government wanted black people to work only at menial jobs, black children were taught very little in schools.

Nelson and his friends had tried everything to change the government's mind. They had begged and pleaded. They had protested and marched. They had defied the laws and they had gone to jail. And still the National Party would not change. Still they insisted that white people were better than black people and deserved more.

Nelson and his friends knew that after all these years of trying, there was only one more option left to them. They would have to shock the National Party. They decided they would have to use violence. They agreed they would not kill innocent people, nor would they fight head-to-head in a war with the government's huge, well-equipped army. Instead they chose sabotage. Sabotage is when you cause as much trouble as you can by blowing up important things, like electricity pylons and railway lines. They thought they might finally persuade the government to listen if the trains didn't run and the phones didn't work. Nelson also thought that if white people and black people were ever to live in peace together, a war which hurt innocent people would not be the right path to follow. Nelson knew his complaint was against the government, not against white people.

Nelson's new job was to build a small, secret army. But it was very dangerous work. If the government caught him, they might very well kill him on the spot. They could also hang him. So now Nelson went about in a disguise, mostly at night. At first he stayed in different places every night. Then he moved to Liliesleaf, to a little cottage on the farm. When he was out and about, he practised being invisible. He tried not to walk as tall or stand as straight. He did not ask for things but waited to be told what to do. He didn't shave or cut his hair. Most people didn't notice him. He called himself David.

He met with people he trusted, others who wanted to end apartheid. He helped them learn how to use explosives and guns. He taught them to make bombs out of paraffin tins and timing devices with ballpoint pens. Some of his followers were sent far away to learn military skills in places like China and Libya.

In December 1961, Nelson received an invitation to attend a conference in Ethiopia, a distant country in far eastern Africa. Nelson was 42 years old and he had never been beyond the borders of his home country, South Africa. He decided to accept the invitation but knew some careful planning would be needed. He didn't want to be caught by the police, who were looking everywhere for him. He couldn't just buy an air ticket and fly out of the country. He would have to find a quiet border post and slip over, hopefully unnoticed. The plan was that Nelson would wait at a secret rendezvous in the township of Soweto. There, some friends, including Walter, would meet him and give him forged travel papers.

Nelson left the farm at the appointed hour, travelled to the secret meeting place and waited. He waited and waited. What he didn't know was that Walter had been arrested by the police on his way to the meeting place. Eventually, Nelson gave up waiting. He would have to move to a new plan. It was only about four or five hours' drive to the next door country of Bechuanaland (which is now called Botswana). He would just have to find another car and someone else to drive. After calling around to some people he knew, he at last found someone who was prepared to drive him to the border. Finally, the trip was underway.

Nelson was very nervous during the long drive from Soweto to the Bechuanaland border. He was worried about being discovered by the police. He was also anxious about leaving his home country for the first time. He could feel his heart racing for what seemed like hours as he watched a burly customs official leaf through his forged travel documents and, finally, mark the last page with an exit stamp. Nelson felt the stress drain away from his insides and his spirits lift as he walked out of the control point building and into the late afternoon sun. He had escaped! He had left his home country for the first time. He was elated.

On the Bechuanaland side of the border Nelson was met by friends and taken into the small, nearby town of Lobatse. He was booked into a hotel and he stayed there for a few days before suddenly being forced to move on. Nelson heard that another member of the ANC had been kidnapped by the South African police and smuggled back across the border. He didn't want that to happen to him. The further away he was from the South African border, the safer he would feel. A small plane was chartered to take him much further north to a town called Kasane. From Kasane, the plan was that he would fly to Tanganyika (now called Tanzania) and then on to Ethiopia.

He felt much less anxious when the chartered plane took off from Lobatse and carried him away up into the skies. After a few hours, the plane was nearing Kasane when the airplane radio crackled into life.

'Airstrip at Kasane is waterlogged, over,' the radio said. 'Please land at the temporary runway five miles east.'

The small plane turned east and Nelson soon spotted a very thin patch of red earth carved into the bush. The plane circled for the landing, touched down in a cloud of dust and bumped to a halt. It taxied to the terminal building, which was only an empty shelter .

'You had better wait in the plane,' the pilot said to Nelson. 'Who knows what might be in the bush.'

Before long, an open truck came up the road. 'Mr Mandela!' the driver called out, 'Sorry I'm late.'

The man jumped out of the truck and came bounding over to the plane. Thanking the pilot, Nelson climbed down the plane's ladder, pulled his suitcase out of the doorway and turned to shake hands with the driver of the truck.

'So sorry again to keep you waiting. There's a herd of rogue elephants just down the road. Had to wait for them to get out of the way. You'll be staying in my hotel. It's not far. Don't mind the guns in the back. They're just in case the elephants decide they don't like us on the way home.'

As Nelson settled in among the guns and bags in the

back of the truck, he noticed a lioness pad lazily out of the bush 50 yards away. He caught his breath. This was the first time Nelson, the African prince, had ever really seen the Africa of myth and legend. He had seen cows, sheep and motor cars before but never antelopes, zebras or lions. Where Nelson had grown up, there were no jungles and very few wild animals. His village was surrounded by farmland, fields and pastures. Once upon a time, wild animals roamed right across Africa. But by the time Nelson was born, many of these animals had been hunted so much that they had all but disappeared.

As they drove to the hotel along the jungle track, Nelson marvelled at the wild game. He especially liked the baboons. The troop of monkeys seemed to fan out through the jungle with military precision.

Early the next morning, Nelson continued on the next stage of his trip. He left Bechuanaland for a small town called Mbeya in Tanganyika. The small plane flew near the amazing Victoria Falls, one of the world's great natural wonders, then north through a mountain range. As the plane buzzed high above the mountain peaks, the weather changed. The cloud became thick and the plane bumped and bounced. Nelson felt like he was riding on a cork in rough seas.

'Mbeya, Mbeya, come in Mbeya,' the pilot kept calling. But there was no response. 'Mbeya, Mbeya,' he shouted. Still nothing.

Rain crashed against the windscreen and the wind buffeted the plane. Pockets of air made the small craft suddenly drop like a stone or soar upwards unexpectedly. The pilot couldn't see a thing. The thick mist turned the whole world into a white blanket. When the pilot couldn't raise the airport at Mbeya, he dropped to a lower altitude and began to follow a road far below which twisted its way through the mountains.

'Mbeya, Mbeya, come in Mbeya,' Nelson heard the pilot say again into his radio.

Then, suddenly, the plane was veering sharply to one side. The engines were roaring. Nelson clung to his seat. 'This is it,' he thought. 'Now I am going to die.' He braced himself for the impact of metal on stone and for the terrible noise which would be the last sound he would hear. But the plane climbed and the engine strained and soon they were safe. Nelson saw the sheer rocky face of a huge mountain which they had only just missed. It had been a very close shave. Then, almost as suddenly as the mist had appeared, the plane burst into bright, clear sunshine. The town of Mbeya was just ahead. As happy as he was to see Mbeya, Nelson would never enjoy flying again.

Still, he notched up thousands of miles on that trip. He went on to visit several African countries including Egypt, Tunisia, Morocco, Sudan, Senegal and Algeria, before flying to Europe.

In London Nelson met many prominent people, from politicians to newspaper editors. It was a special treat for him to see the Houses of Parliament. While he hated Britain's colonial past, he loved much about the country. It was the home of parliamentary democracy. And, for Nelson, the English gentleman was the very model of manners and style.

One of the highlights of his trip was when he met up again with his old friend Oliver Tambo. Oliver had been his partner in the law firm in Johannesburg, but some time ago he had gone into exile, which means he had left his own country and didn't know if he would ever be allowed back. He was now in charge of the ANC office in London. His job was to teach the world about what was happening in South Africa, and to build support for the ANC's fight against apartheid.

All too soon, Nelson's trip was coming to an end. He had time for one last vital task. He needed to learn how to become a real soldier. And if he wanted to be a soldier, he needed to know how to shoot a gun, how to make a bomb and plan an attack. To learn these skills he went back to Ethiopia, to the headquarters of the Ethiopian Riot Battalion, in the capital Addis Ababa.

Ethiopia had once been a colony of Italy. The Ethiopians had successfully fought their own guerrilla war for independence from Italy so they had much to teach. In Addis Ababa, Nelson was taught the art and science of soldiering. He was given lectures on military strategy and on discipline. He learned how to use an automatic rifle and a handgun. He went on long marches and was taught how to command an army.

Soon, though, Nelson received word that the ANC needed him urgently. It was time to return home.

He slipped back into South Africa the same way he had left. The police were enraged. They knew he had been travelling the world, but they couldn't catch him. As for Nelson, he went straight back to work, and continued with his plan of building a guerrilla army to fight a war of sabotage against the South African government. This made the police more determined than ever to catch him. They issued a warrant for his arrest and Nelson became the most wanted man in South Africa. A new law was passed making sabotage punishable by death. Still they couldn't catch him. Sometimes Nelson called up the newspapers after a lucky escape to taunt the police, which only made them even madder. Nelson became known as the 'Black Pimpernel', named after a character from a famous book who was never caught. The whole nation wondered where he was and whether or not he would make another lucky escape.

During these hard years, Nelson remarried. After the failure of his marriage to Evelyn, he met another young woman with whom he fell in love and, when his divorce from Evelyn was finalised, he married her. Her name was Nomzamo Winnifred Madikizela, but everyone knew her as Winnie.

Winnie was a social worker, one of the first black female social workers to work at the huge state hospital near Nelson's home in Orlando. She was a strong, clever, beautiful woman and Nelson knew immediately he wanted her to be his wife. He asked her to marry him on their first date.

Their marriage was far from normal. Both Winnie and Nelson were committed to politics. They were always at meetings, or helping to organise strikes and protests, and they were put in jail on several occasions.

But they did find time to have children. By 1962, they had two little girls, Zindzi and Zeni. While Nelson was living in the cottage at Lilisleaf, Winnie and the girls would visit him from time to time.

Nelson's luck held out for almost two years. The sabotage was going well and many explosions had taken place. Then, one day, Nelson's luck ran out. He was caught. On Monday 15 October 1962, Nelson appeared in court to answer charges of leaving the country illegally and of helping to organise an illegal strike. Later, the charge of sabotage was added.

Nelson's trial is very famous. It is called the Rivonia trial because Liliesleaf Farm was in Rivonia and that is where Nelson was living and where many of his friends were also caught. It is famous because instead of defending himself, Nelson stood up and told the court of his beliefs. Dressed in the cloak and beads of a Thembu prince, Nelson rose to speak in the ornate, high-ceilinged courtroom at the Palace of Justice in Pretoria.

He said: 'In my youth... I listened to the elders of my tribe telling stories of the old days. Amongst the tales they related to me were those of wars fought by our ancestors in defence of the fatherland. The names of Bambatha and Makanna.... were praised as the pride and glory of the entire African nation. I hoped then that life might offer me the opportunity to serve my people and make my own humble contribution to their freedom struggle. This is what has motivated me in all that I have done.'

Nelson told the court that for 50 years the ANC had been struggling peacefully for all people to be treated the same, black and white. They had tried everything. But they had achieved nothing. Sabotage was the only option left which did not involve bloodshed.

Nelson finished his speech with famous words that echoed around the whole world: 'During my lifetime I have dedicated myself to this struggle of the African people. I have fought against white domination and I have fought against black domination. I have cherished the ideal of a democratic and free society in which all persons live together in harmony and with equal opportunities. It is an ideal which I hope to live for and to achieve. But if needs be, it is an ideal for which I am prepared to die.'

Nelson was not sentenced to death. As we have heard, he was sentenced to life in jail – partly because the government was afraid of making an example of him; Mandela and his fellow activists were now quite well known in the world outside, and the National Party did not want to risk other governments in other countries becoming involved in the way they were running South Africa.

Nevertheless, Robben Island was no ordinary jail. It was the toughest, cruellest jail around.

CHAPTER SEVEN

Nelson sat in the courtyard of the old fortress with a six-pound hammer in his hand. The harsh sun beat down on his shoulders. He reached behind him and picked up a large piece of stone, placed it between his knees and then smashed the rock with the hammer. Sharp chips sprayed everywhere. Again he brought the hammer down. Big chunks of rock cracked off the main piece. The perspiration dripped off his face. Again and again he hit until all that was left of the big piece of rock was a pile of gravel. He reached behind him and found another rock. He raised the hammer once more.

'Silence,' shouted a prison guard to two whispering prisoners. Above the toiling men, another guard patrolled on the wall, a shotgun on his shoulder and a fierce guard dog straining at the leash in his hand.

The prisoners sat in four rows. The thuds of their hammers were the only noises. Each prisoner had a large pile of rocks behind him. They held the rocks in place with a strip of old tyre rubber tied into a loop. All day the prisoners pounded the rocks into smaller and smaller pieces. The gravel was then collected in wheelbarrows and dumped into an enormous skip. When the skip was full it was taken away and an empty one was brought in to the courtyard. The prisoners took only a short break at midday to eat a soup which smelled horrid, then it was back to the rocks once more.

Nelson wondered how long he would be able to do this. He couldn't imagine spending the rest of his life breaking rocks with a hammer. But that is what his life had become. It was enough to make anyone want to curl up and die. It was enough to fill anyone with anger and hatred. When it rained, he sat breaking rocks in the courtyard. In the sun, he did the same. Whether he shivered with cold or burned in the heat, hour after hour, in utter silence, this was where his protests and his dreams had brought him.

But Nelson refused to despair and he refused to hate. He knew that one day he would feel the grass under his feet once more. One day, he would walk free in the sunshine and sleep in his own bed. How he dreamed of that day!

Nelson also knew that he was needed to help fight. A different fight had begun on the island. It was still a fight against apartheid, or so he figured. But this wasn't a fight that would take place in a courtroom, or even in the streets. This was a battle for dignity. It was a fight to wear long trousers instead of shorts, to be treated with respect by the warders, to get better food and to have more study time.

When Nelson refused to wear shorts or eat the terrible food, he was thrown in a cell all by himself. This was called solitary confinement. During these times, he was not allowed to talk to anyone at all. He was allowed to eat only rice-water, the water left over from boiling rice. He was totally isolated. Soon every hour seemed like a year. Nelson had nothing to read and nothing to write on or with. His mind began to turn in on itself. He desperately wanted something to focus on. He began to relish the presence even of insects in his lonely cell. He found himself wanting to drop down on his hands and knees to begin conversations with a cockroach.

The enemy in prison was the warders. They were mostly young, white Afrikaner men who believed what they had been taught: that black people were worth much less than white people. Nelson refused to think that the warders were all bad, even when they were at their most cruel. He knew that in every single person there is something good. He knew if he could touch their hearts, they would change. He decided as soon as he arrived on Robben Island that he would try to reach out to the warders. He talked to them. He never allowed them to treat him badly. If they needed help with legal matters like contracts or if they wanted to get married or buy a home, Nelson would help them as if they were his clients in his old law firm.

There were always cruel warders who tried to punish or humiliate Nelson. But he had great inner strength as well as a knowledge of the law. 'If you so much as lay a hand on me,' he told one bullying warder, 'I will take you to the highest court in the land and when I finish with you, you will be as poor as a church mouse.' The warder left Nelson alone.

Nelson learned to read novels and poetry in the Afrikaner language, which was called Afrikaans. He spoke to the warders in Afrikaans. His fellow prisoners looked on in amazement. They wondered what he was up to. Nelson knew that one day, he would be free and leading his people again. He realised that if there was to be real peace in South Africa, someone needed to understand the Afrikaners. They wouldn't just go away. They were descendents of people who had lived on the southern tip of Africa for more than 300 years. There could be no future without them. Someone needed to reach out to them, even make friends with them. He thought that if he could win the trust and respect of Afrikaner prison warders, he would learn a great deal about Afrikaners in general. If he could learn about the hopes and fears of Afrikaners, he could soothe these fears and they could seek a path towards peace together. Sooner or later, everybody would need to learn to get on. There was simply no other way. Without peace, there would be war. Millions of people could die in such a war. The country would be dragged into a dark pit of violence and hatred. It would be black against white, Afrikaner against African, perhaps forever.

Nelson knew there had to be another way. He believed in his heart that in spite of everything the Afrikaners, the government and other white people had done to him, he must forgive them. Only with forgiveness and understanding could he reach out for the hand of his enemy and turn him into a friend. Some of the warders grew to respect and love Nelson so much they became lifelong friends.

After he had been on the island for six months, Nelson was told a visitor would be coming to see him the next day. He spent the rest of the day and all night hoping and praying it would be his dear wife, Winnie. The next morning he was led to the prison's visiting room. The room was cramped and had no windows. It had a row of cubicles on either side of a large panel of glass. The prisoners sat in a row on one side of the glass and their visitors sat in a row on the other side.

As Nelson sat down in a cubicle, he saw Winnie and his heart soared. But he could see from her face that life was hard for her and their two little girls. Winnie herself was a 'banned' person. It had not been easy to arrange a visit. The glass was so thick and the holes drilled through it so small that Nelson and Winnie had to shout to hear one another.

Behind Nelson stood three prison warders. Another two stood behind Winnie.

'Who are you talking about?' the warders asked from time to time. Nelson and Winnie were only allowed to speak about their immediate family members, nobody else. Time and again the warders interrupted. It felt as if they had barely been there a moment when one of the warders said: 'Time up! Time up!'. The 30-minute visit had gone by in a flash. Nelson and Winnie would not see each other again for two years.

Nelson kept a picture of Winnie by his bed. Each morning he kissed the picture and rubbed his nose against hers. He tried to imagine she was really there, right in front of him, as close as the picture. He desperately looked forward to receiving a letter from her and treasured them when they arrived. When the other prisoners got letters from their loved ones and Nelson didn't, he felt as empty as the desert. Nelson was allowed to write and receive only one letter and see only one visitor every six months. Sometimes the prison guards decided to be cruel and lost his letters from Winnie on purpose.

One morning, instead of sitting in the courtyard smashing rocks, the prisoners were given a new task. They were marched out of the prison, into a truck, and they were driven to a place where a large white crater had been cut into the rocky hillside. The cliffs of the crater were blindingly white. At the bottom there were a few old metal sheds. This was a limestone quarry. Nelson was told they would work in the quarry for six months. In fact, it would be 13 years before their work there ended.

Soon, instead of driving to the quarry, the prisoners marched. At least during the marches Nelson could see something of the island. He could smell the eucalyptus blossoms and, sometimes, he spotted a deer grazing in the distance. Even in the quarry he could see birds flitting overhead and he could feel the breeze blowing off the ocean. That was much better than sitting in a grey prison cell. Things had already started to improve. But Nelson never gave up hoping that one day he would be free.

There were more than 30 political prisoners who were all kept together on Robben Island and more arrived all the time. Some of them could barely read or write, others had advanced degrees. They all believed apartheid was wrong and had given their lives to fighting it.

They used their time in jail together to study. They taught each other and helped each other to learn. They also had fierce arguments about almost anything. One of the worst arguments was about whether there were tigers in Africa. Some said there were, others said there weren't. They also talked about more serious things, like how to beat the political system they hated so much and what they would do if they won. They wanted to keep their minds sharp and be ready for when they were released. Nelson was pleased that at least he was in prison with friends like Walter.

Led by Nelson, the prisoners stood up to the guards. They clung fiercely to their dignity and their pride. They stopped eating until the food got better. They complained about the prison. Sometimes they won, sometimes they lost. Punishment was severe and often meant endless days in solitary confinement. Hard-won privileges like access to books or writing materials were taken away for the smallest of reasons. Survival was a daily struggle.

The prisoners' job in the quarry was to dig out the limestone – the layers of old, crusty seashells and coral between the rock – with a pickaxe and then shovel it into wheelbarrows. It was hard work made harder by the piercing brightness of the white cliffs. By the end of the day they were not only exhausted, they were covered in fine white dust from top to toe. They looked like ghosts as they marched back to the prison. The chips and dust of limestone constantly got in their eyes. Nelson and many of the prisoners had problems with their eyes for the rest of their lives. The prisoners worked in the quarry for three years before they were allowed sun -glasses to shield their eyes from the damaging glare.

In 1969 Nelson's mother Nosekeni Fanny came to visit him. It had been many years since he had seen her and she looked very frail and ill. Nelson felt sad he had not been able to look after her better. After Nelson had left the Great Place, his mother had continued to live in a mud hut in Qunu. Nelson had looked after his mother while he worked as an attorney. But in jail, he had not been able to care for her. He had not been able to send her money for clothes or food. And now she lived in terrible poverty. A few months after her visit to see Nelson in jail, Nosekeni Fanny died. She never really understood why her son had chosen politics at the expense of his own family. This gnawed at Nelson's conscience. Had he made the right choice in putting the welfare of his people before that of his family?

More bad news was to come. Nelson heard in May than Winnie had been put in jail. He felt helpless and sad. He then learned that his eldest child, his son Thembi, had been killed in a car accident. Nelson was not allowed to go either to his mother's funeral or to his son's. He was deeply sorrowful. He felt as if there was a hole in his heart, a hole that could never be filled. And yet still he forgave and dreamed of a brighter future.

Each day was the same for Nelson: He got up at 5:30am, cleaned his cell and rolled up his mat and blankets. Breakfast was at 6:45am. It was a thin porridge served in old metal drums in the courtyard. After a cell inspection, it was off to the limestone quarry for the rest of the morning. Lunch was taken at the quarry. It was a drink of corn powder and yeast. After lunch, work continued at the quarry until 4pm. At this hour the guards blew shrill whistles and the prisoners were lined up and inspected. Then it was back to the prison for a half hour clean-up with cold sea-water. There was no hot water on Robben Island for the prisoners and the bitterly cold sea-water never got all the dust off. In winter, washing in it was torture.

At 4:30pm, supper was delivered to the cells. It was usually porridge, sometimes with a vegetable. Every other day there was a small piece of meat which was mostly gristle. At 8pm, the prisoners were ordered to sleep. The lights were never turned out. A single light bulb burned in Nelson's cell all day and all night.

It was the same every day. Each day was like the last and each week just like the one before it. Soon the months and the years blended into each other. None of the prisoners were allowed to wear watches, but Nelson drew a calendar on his wall. He thought it important to keep track of the time. For many years, the prisoners were not allowed newspapers nor even a radio. Time itself seemed to slow down. The days seemed endless. A request for a new toothbrush could take six months. The minutes went by like years. The years went by like minutes. An afternoon pounding rocks seemed like forever, but suddenly it was Christmas again and the year had gone. In a flash, five years had passed. Then ten more had gone. Then another year. And another.

'How much longer?' Nelson wondered. 'How much longer before I am free?'.

CHAPTER EIGHT

Slowly, life on the island began to get better. Instead of going to work in the quarry, Nelson and the other political prisoners were sent to the beach every day to collect seaweed. The seaweed was shipped to countries like Japan where it was used as fertiliser. Nelson and his friends gathered the seaweed into big piles. Sometimes they waded out into the icy Atlantic to fetch it. On cold days, this was a nasty chore. But Nelson far preferred being on the beach to working in the quarry.

The food got better too. For lunch, they picked mussels, clams and abalone off the rocks. They even teased lobsters out of their hiding places in the shallows. They made big pots of seafood stew which tasted wonderful. Even the warders, who were getting friendlier all the time, were given some. Sometimes the warders and the prisoners ate together on the rocks in the sunshine.

Nelson loved hearing the seabirds calling out over-head, smelling the salty waves crashing on the shore and seeing the huge container ships drift by. He thought all the time of escaping, especially when he looked out over the bay to the glinting towers of the city of Cape Town. But it was too far to swim in freezing, shark-infested waters. Nelson remembered that, in all the hundreds of years Robben Island had been a prison, very few people had ever escaped and survived. The prisoners thought of many different escape plans, but none could be made to work. Sometimes, Nelson thought the authorities want-ed him to try to escape so they could kill him.

One young warder, recently arrived on the island, told Nelson he had planned an escape for him. He said one night he would drug the guards and give Nelson a key to escape his section. Nelson was told there would be a boat waiting for him near the lighthouse. On the boat would be scuba-diving gear which Nelson would use to swim to the harbour. From there, he would be taken to a local airport and flown out of the country.

Nelson thought the plan was far-fetched and didn't trust the new warder. Fortunately, he decided not to try the escape, for he learned later that the warder was an agent for the Bureau of State Security (BOSS), the secret police. The real plan was that Nelson would be killed in a dramatic shoot-out at the airport as he tried to leave the country.

In one corner of the prison courtyard, Nelson was allowed to start a vegetable garden. It was only small, but he could once again enjoy planting chillies, tomatoes and radishes and watch them grow. Not all the prisoners on the island came from the same political party as Nelson. Many didn't believe the same things as him even though they agreed on the need to fight the government. Nelson made a special effort to talk to these prisoners. He looked for things they could agree on, things they had in common. Then he thought of things they could do together. He knew you didn't have to agree on every little thing to work as a team. Sometimes it was good if everybody thought about something in a different way.

On the island, Nelson became the undisputed leader of the prisoners. Even the warders grew to respect him. In the world outside, too, he was becoming famous. Many people wanted Nelson to be released from prison. A 'Free Mandela' campaign was launched which spread to many countries. Nelson wrote to the South African president, P.W. Botha, pleading with him to talk about the future of the country.

Then, in June 1976, terrible violence broke out in South Africa after the government tried to force all students to receive their education in Afrikaans. Over the next ten years this violence grew worse and worse. The government threw thousands of people in prison and brought in ever harsher laws. Many people looked to Nelson for leadership, even though he had been locked away on a small island in the Atlantic for almost two decades.

Nelson continued to amaze the other prisoners as well as his visitors with his willingness to forgive. Once, he was stopped from studying for three years after he was found reading a newspaper discarded carelessly by a warder. Still he refused to be bitter. However bad things got, he knew others were suffering more. When he felt sad about his small cell, he thought of the young man just arrived who had been tortured by the police. When his feet were cold, he thought of the man without feet.

Nelson found it harder to be strong when he heard of the horrible things happening to his family. For seven years, Winnie and their two daughters, Zindzi and Zeni, had been banished to the small, distant town of

Brandfort, 250 miles from their home in Orlando. Few people there spoke Winnie's language, which made daily life extremely lonely.

The tiny house where they were dumped had no heating and no running water. The toilet was outside.

Whenever she could, Winnie wrote to Nelson. Every six months, she went to see him if the prison authorities allowed it. Sometimes she took the children, but only after they had turned 16 years old.

Nelson was never allowed to touch her or the children. But it made him happy to see them through the glass and to hear the latest family news. Nelson was angry but he refused to hate. Part of what gave him his strength was that he knew he was right and believed in what he was fighting for. At night, when he lay in bed, he counted his blessings, one by one. He had a wife who loved him. His children were growing up and had started having children of their own. His friend Oliver Tambo was working tirelessly to build the ANC. His other friend Walter was by his side every day. The world was supporting his struggle. There were always things to be grateful for, even in prison. He kept pushing the government to talk. He wrote letters and sent messages.

Then, in April 1982, the head of Robben Island

prison came into Nelson's cell. 'It is time to pack your bags,' he told Nelson.

'You are leaving the island.' Nelson had been on the island for 18 years. Now it was time to go. Within hours, he was on a small boat chugging through the swelling waves. Nelson was not set free. Instead he was moved to a new prison. It was a prison on the mainland in which he had a bigger room, a real bed and a roof garden. He was given better food. After Robben Island it felt like a five-star hotel but there was no view other than concrete walls.

South Africa was by now in turmoil and the government was desperate. It wanted to hear Nelson's ideas. What could he do to stop the war between the police and the people? What did he want? Senior government ministers came to see him.

On one occasion, Nelson was taken to meet the Prime Minister, P.W. Botha. Nelson explained over and over: The war would end when every person was treated the same, whether they were black or white. It would end when every person helped to make decisions together, just like the Thembu at their councils. It would end when every child, no matter what colour they were, could go to any school, live in any house and grow up to be anything they wanted. It would end when every political prisoner, like Nelson, was set free. Only then would there be peace.

But still Nelson sat in jail.

In January 1989, P.W. Botha fell ill. He was replaced by a new leader of the ruling National Party, F.W. De Klerk. There were hopes in South Africa and internationally that De Klerk would be a different kind of leader. Perhaps he would be the one to change things?

When De Klerk took up office, the country was consumed by violence and by civil war. The economy was in tatters. The world treated South Africa as an outcast, a pariah. The United Nations had declared apartheid a crime against humanity. The new leader knew things had to change. And he knew only one person could help.

CHAPTER NINE

At 4pm on Sunday 11 February 1990, Nelson walked free from prison. He had been behind bars for 10,000 days. Put in jail in his prime at 42 years old, he was now an old man in his seventies. His children had grown up and started their own families. His body had aged and his eyes weren't so good anymore. He walked with a slight limp.

Nelson had thought there might be a few people waiting at the gate of the prison to welcome him. He could not believe his eyes when he saw a crowd of thousands, cheering and yelling. Television cameras, reporters and photographers from around the world swarmed around him. Everyone wanted to know: 'What does it feel like, Mandela, to be free?'.

Nelson couldn't say. The feeling was too big. You

couldn't describe it in a word or two. He had waited too many years. He had suffered too much. He had yearned for this moment for too long. He held Winnie's hand as he walked out of jail and waved.

Nelson had daydreamed so often of this day, the day he was set free: he would go home to his small house in Orlando, eat a special meal with his wife, children and grandchildren, and then sleep in his own bed. But the dream was not to be. There were simply too many people to see. There was simply much too much to do.

Nelson soon got down to business. It was time to talk. And talk. For four years Nelson talked. He talked to his friends at the African National Congress, the party he joined all those years ago. He talked to the Afrikaners in the government. He talked to white people and he talked to black people. Everywhere, people were amazed that Nelson was able to forgive and talk with the people who had put him in jail for 27 years, banished his wife, broken his family, tortured and killed his friends. It wasn't the people who did that, Nelson said. It was apartheid which had been put in place, brick by brick, over the previous 300 years.

At times, it seemed as if the talks would end in disaster and the country would fall into war and chaos. At other times, it seemed success was almost within Nelson's grasp. He had in his mind a vision of what things should be like. It was a picture in which his country belonged to everyone who lived in it, in which everyone could go to school and in which everyone, black and white, young and old, men and women, could work and play as equals.

The government leader, F.W. De Klerk, said he was worried that white people would not be welcome if black people took over the government. But Nelson said the country badly needed the white people and begged them to stay. Just as he had always maintained in prison, Nelson now insisted that there was good in everybody. The Afrikaners were astonished by how much Nelson knew about their history. They were touched he could talk their language. They were relieved when he understood what worried them most. Ever so slowly, by giving a little here and taking a bit there, by working hard and by talking, the fists of anger opened up to become hands of friendship.

***

Nelson became the President of South Africa on 10 May

1994. It was the first time that everybody living in the country, black and white, had been allowed to choose their leaders and vote in an election. By far the most people chose Nelson. It was the first time Nelson himself had ever voted. It was also the first time that South Africa had a black president. F.W. De Klerk became Nelson's deputy and they ruled together. A miracle had happened. Together they had guided a people on the edge of war to a new time of hope and equality. Someone called this new country the 'rainbow nation'. Just like a rainbow, it was made up of lots of different colours. Just like a rainbow, all the colours joined together were more beautiful than any one colour alone.

What happened in South Africa gave everyone in the world hope. If Nelson could forgive and embrace his enemy, this could happen in other places, too. Suddenly it seemed there was no conflict in the world which, with a little Nelson Mandela magic, could not be turned to love and friendship. A man who had spent 27 years in a jail cell had succeeded in giving the whole world hope: hope that good will always prevail, hope that enemies can learn to live together, hope that even though we may look different we are really all the same.

For five years, Nelson served as the President of South

Africa. He travelled all over the world spreading his message of hope and forgiveness. At home, little by little, life got better for his people.

Whenever he can, he goes back to the small village of Qunu where he grew up all those years ago. He loves to see the green hills of his childhood and hear the burbling of the icy streams as they cut through the valley. He has built a house near the Great Place where the Regent once lived and where he and Justice shared a hut. He still chats with the elders and gives them wise counsel as they gather under the bluegum trees. And, if the children living nearby are very lucky, they catch Nelson during one of his long walks and slip their hand in his. Or they find him sitting by the fire. It doesn't take much to persuade him to tell amazing stories of faraway places and strange people. Their eyes light up, just like Nelson's did when he was a child, as they dream of the day when they too might get the chance to become a hero with evil to fight and a people to save.

Key Dates

1918 – Born at Qunu in the Transkei region of South Africa, July 18

1940 – Expelled from Fort Hare University

1944 – Helped establish the African National Congress (ANC) Youth League; married Evelyn Mase

1950 – Became ANC Youth League President

1952 – Elected National Volunteer-in-Chief in the Defiance Campaign; opened first black law firm in South Africa with Oliver Tambo

1958 – Married Nomzamo Winnifred Madikizela (Winnie)

1960 – Detained when ANC banned after the Sharpeville massacre; established armed wing of the ANC, Umkhonto weSizwe (Spear of the Nation)

1962 – Left South Africa to undergo military training. On his return, he was arrested, convicted and jailed for five years for leaving the country illegally and for inciting others to strike.

1964 – Sentenced to life in prison for sabotage at the Rivonia Trial; went to Robben Island

1990 – Released after 27 years in jail on Sunday 11 February

1991 – Became President of the ANC
1994 – Became President of South Africa
1998 – Marries Graca Machel
1999 – Retires from public life

FURTHER READING FOR ADULTS:

Long Walk to Freedom – The Autobiography of Nelson Mandela, Macdonald Purnell Limited, Randburg, South Africa, 1994.

Mandela – The Authorised Biography, by Anthony Sampson, HarperCollins, London, 1999.